PROJECT MANAGEMENT LITE

*Just Enough to
Get the Job Done
...Nothing More*

JUANA CLARK CRAIG, PMP

COLUMBIA, MARYLAND

ISBN: 1478129220
ISBN-13: 9781478129226

Library of Congress Control Number: 2012912115
CreateSpace, North Charleston, SC

First Edition, 2012

Published in the United States of America

Dedication

This book is dedicated to my husband, Keith; my daughter, Alex; my son, Donny; and my stepson, Shawn.

Everything should be made as simple as possible, but not simpler.

− Albert Einstein

Disclaimer

Every effort has been made to make this book as complete and as accurate as possible. It is sold with the understanding that the publisher and author are not engaged in rendering legal, accounting, or other professional services.

It is not the purpose of this book to rehash all the information that is otherwise available. The purposes of this book are to educate and to entertain. The author and publisher disclaim any personal liability, either directly or indirectly, for advice or information presented within.

Contents

Introduction

Got projects that need to get done as quickly and efficiently as possible *without* requiring a master's degree in project management?

Project Management Lite™ is a minimalistic approach to the project management process that can help you complete your projects *fast*, without all the confusing mumbo-jumbo of traditional project management techniques.

Whether you just need to get through this one project (with your sanity intact) or are looking to learn project management skills to boost your resume, Project Management Lite has you covered.

Whom this book is for

This book is for you or your organization if:

*   Your projects are overtaking your to-do list, but you're not sure how to tackle them most efficiently or even where to *start*.

- You have a just-the-basics-please approach to project management. You don't need everything under the sun, just enough to get you through.

- You find the typical project management language and concepts confusing, "heavy," and total overkill for what you need to complete the project at hand.

- You suddenly find yourself in charge of a project that needs managing, but you and/or your staff have little or no project management training or skills (and no time to master them!).

- You're a beginner and want to learn some basic information about project management (but not so much that you'll feel completely overloaded right off the bat).

- You want to boost your skills so you can move into a new career or go after a long-overdue promotion.

- You want to learn a simple, easy-to-use, easy-to-understand, and minimalistic approach to getting projects done well.

- Your last project was a chaotic mess, and you want to avoid THAT mayhem again at all costs.

The bottom line:

You want just enough to get the job done. Nothing more.

You're not alone

Here's the reality of the situation for most businesses and organizations when it comes to project management:

- They have projects they need to get done, but they are not sure where to start.

- They know they need project management but aren't overly disciplined when it comes to process.

- They find that the language and concepts are confusing, "heavy," and overkill for what they need to do.

- Most of their projects are small to medium sized and don't require a heavy-duty, professional consultant–laden process.

- They have little or no project management training or skills.

- They have been through one of those "heavy" project management training classes but still don't know what to do.

- They want a simple, easy-to-use, easy-to-understand, and easy-to-implement approach to managing projects.

Many people are in the same boat. They need or want project management but want just enough to get the job done—nothing more.

Enter Project Management Lite

Project Management Lite, or PM Lite for short, is based on over twenty-five years of project management experience as well as training, mentoring, and coaching new and experienced project managers. You know them. They are the ones who are available—or YOU.

PM Lite is based on how I have seen organizations actually run their projects and how I have trained others to run theirs. It focuses on three tasks: clearly defining the project and plan, working the plan until it's done and closing it out.

Where it all started

Way back in the late 1990s, I was the head of the first project management office for a *Fortune* 500 corporation. (A project management office helps an organization with project management training and mentoring.)

"Give us a project management process and make it good" was the pronouncement from on high. So I went forth and worked with my team. We searched, and we wrote, and we developed an outstanding project management process complete with everything for every size project including the kitchen sink. It was a thing of beauty.

Management sang our praises and pronounced it great. They proclaimed, "Now go forth and teach the masses!" And so we did. We trained the executives, the leaders, and the staff.

The masses received our wisdom and called it "great!" And then they said, "Now just tell us the minimum amount we have to do to get the job done."

And so I did.

PM Lite Overview

Making the simple complicated is commonplace; making the complicated simple, awesomely simple, that's creativity.

—Charles Mingus

Just Enough to Get the Job Done

Tag, you're it

Your boss drops by to chat. "I have an opportunity for you. I have a project that I need you to run."

"But I've never run a project before," you say.

"Don't worry. You'll figure it out," your boss says, patting you on the shoulder. "Just don't screw it up."

Now what? Where in the world are you supposed to start?

Let's start with some basics

What makes something a project anyway?

Before we start thinking about how to run a project, let's talk about what makes something a project. Here are the things that make a project a project:

3

- It has a start and an end; it doesn't go on forever.

- It's focused on achieving an outcome.

- It involves putting together a sequence of steps that goes from the start to the end and creates the outcome.

- It might have a budget, an amount of money set aside to cover the costs.

- It may require a team of people to work on it or it could just be you.

What kinds of things can be projects?

Pretty much *anything* can be a project. Projects can be very small and simple, very large and complex, or anything in between. They can be business-/work-related or personal.

Here are some examples of things, both business and personal, that could be considered projects:

- Launching a new product

- Setting up a new organization

- Revamping a process

- Planning a graduation party

- Planning your vacation

- Achieving a goal

Who runs the project?

The person who runs the project is called the "project manager." A project manager is in charge of making sure everything gets done. He or she does what is called "project management."

What is "project management"?

Project management is simply a process for getting things done. Project management helps you define what you need to do, plan it out, and get it done.

Project management can go from very light and simple to very heavy and complex, depending on the size and complexity of what you're trying to do. Usually heavy and complex projects come with professional consultants attached. (Consultants are people whom businesses pay lots and lots of money to run their projects for them.)

Project management comes with its own language—phrases like "pert charts," "earned value," blah, blah! No wonder people get intimidated and confused. The words alone are enough to make your head spin.

Where does PM Lite fit in?

PM Lite takes the project management process and breaks it down into three basic process areas:

1. Plan the project.

2. Work the plan.

3. Close it out.

Plan the project

This process area is about clearly defining what you're trying to do, what the goal is, and what the outcome(s) should be, and then coming up with a realistic plan to get you from start to finish.

Here are the steps to planning the project:

- Define what you're trying to do.

- Come up with a plan to do it.

Work the plan

This process area is about actually working through the plan and ensuring that the work gets done and that the plan, team, problems, and communications needed to achieve the outcome are managed.

Here are the steps to working the plan:

- Get everyone focused.

- Make sure the work gets done.

- Handle the problems.

- Deal with any changes.

- Keep everyone informed.

- Manage the team.

Close it out

This process makes sure the end result gets turned over to whoever asked for it, that any outstanding problems are handled, that everything is wrapped up, and that the team members are thanked for their involvement.

Here are the steps to closing the project:

- Wrap it up.

- Celebrate.

Less process, faster results

Traditional project management consists of five process areas and forty-two processes. With PM Lite, you get three process areas and ten processes. And depending on whether or not you have a team, your project could involve even fewer processes.

Everything is explained in plain English so that you can stop spinning your wheels, stop drowning in the project management process, or stop getting lost in a bunch of complicated tools.

For which projects can you use it?

Individuals have successfully used PM Lite with many types of projects including work, business, and personal projects.

Does it work?

Yes! It does work. The last organization that I worked with and that implemented this process went from a project success rate of below 40 percent to over 95 percent in two years.

Inside the book

First, you'll find the book small and easy to read. A book about light project management shouldn't be a heavy read.

It's short on fluff and long on practical how-to's, with a little humor thrown in for good measure. (After all, project management can be quite boring!)

The book goes into detail for each step of the process and even includes a section on what you can do to help yourself be successful.

The included worksheets and checklists reduce the guesswork and make things even easier.

Come to the Lite Side

So there you have it. If you're truly interested in learning to achieve great results without struggling with cumbersome and overwhelming processes, then step inside.

Where to Start

No one lives long enough to learn everything they need to learn starting from scratch. To be successful, we absolutely, positively have to find people who have already paid the price to learn the things that we need to learn to achieve our goals.

—Brian Tracy

Your Quick Start Guide

Before we jump in, let's look at your project and decide just how much project management you really need. Remember that you want just enough to get the job done.

The length of your project, whether or not you will have a team of people working with you, and whom the project is for will help you determine where to focus.

(Just a quick note: If your project is particularly large and complex, then you may wish to consult other project management books that go more in depth about how to manage those types of projects.)

PM Lite Quick Start Checklist

Don't do anything you don't have to do.

—Louis Fried

If you need to get started quickly, here is the absolute minimum you need to get you started. Each step is defined in more detail in the upcoming sections.

☐ **Define what you're trying to do:** Write up as much as you need—depending on the size, complexity, and duration of the project—to define what the project is about, the goals and outcomes, what has to be delivered, etc. Keep it SMARTER (<u>s</u>pecific, <u>m</u>easurable, <u>a</u>greed upon, <u>r</u>ealistic, <u>t</u>ime bound, <u>e</u>thical, <u>r</u>esourced). Get this reviewed and approved by your boss or customer. *(See Step 1: Define what you're trying to do.)*

☐ **Come up with a plan to do it:** If you will need a team, get together people who will be helping you. Brainstorm and come up with the big chunks of work that need to happen to get the end result. Break each chunk down into smaller pieces, guesstimate how long each part will take, and assign specific people to get it done. Write it down: what has to be done, who's doing it, and when it needs to be done. Make sure all participants are clear about what they need to do, and then get started! *(See Step 2: Come up with a plan to do it; Step 3: Get everyone focused.)*

☐ **Work through the plan:** Make sure that the work is getting done, that problems and changes are being handled, and that information is being shared in a timely manner:

- Are things finishing on time or not?

- Are you handling the problems and changes as they come?

- Are all participants doing what they are supposed to do?

(See Step 4: Make sure the work gets done; Step 5: Handle the problems; Step 6: Deal with any changes; Step 7: Manage the team.)

☐ **Keep everyone informed:** Keep everyone aware of project progress even if it's just an e-mail with an update. *(Step 8: Keep everyone informed.)*

☐ **Wrap it up:** Make sure everything is done and then turn the results/ outcome over to your boss or customer. Review how things went so you do better the next time. Thank everyone for a job well done. *(See Step 9: Wrap it up; Step 10: Celebrate.)*

Plan the Project

You got to be careful if you don't know where you're going,
because you might not get there.

—Yogi Berra

Step 1 – Define What You're Trying to Do

You have to know what you want to get it.

—*Gertrude Stein*

First things first

One of the first things you need to figure out is what the project is all about. What's the goal or outcome of the project? What problem is it trying to solve or what opportunity is it trying to create? What are the boundaries?

It helps to develop a common understanding of the project with the people who want it, those who will be impacted by it, and your team.

You create a clear and focused vision of what is to be achieved, what the general timeframe is, who needs to be involved, what the overall budget is, etc.

If you don't have a clear definition of the project, then you're essentially flying blind.

Where to start

The first thing you need to do is meet with the sponsor and find out as much as you can about what the sponsor wants or needs.

What—and who—is a project sponsor?

First, let's talk about what a sponsor is. The project sponsor is the person who is asking for the project to be completed.

Typically, sponsors also control the money and people, and they may even be the senior end customers. Or they may be the heads of the area that will get whatever it is that your project is delivering. Or they may be those who came up with the idea in the first place.

They can be very senior in the organization or not so senior. In terms of where they are in the organization, it doesn't really matter, provided that the people who need to take action respect their decisions.

Ideally, they will be well positioned to iron out any internal politics for you and will have the ear of people who matter. They must also be able to share information that may be important to your project or team.

People in the sponsor role usually have many different demands on their time, and your project may not be on top of their list, especially if they became sponsors by default.

The sponsor might not have ever been a sponsor before and therefore might not know what is involved. If the sponsor doesn't know what to do, you can be sure he or she won't be able to make the time to find out.

What do you need to know about the project?

Answering the following questions will help you to define the project clearly:

What's the goal or outcome of the project?

You are doing this project to create some sort of outcome.

In talking with sponsor, identify the project's goals. What specific goals is the project to achieve? Goals should be written so that they are SMARTER and understood by all the stakeholders:

Specific – You must know the who, what, where, when, why of the goal.

Measurable – You must be able to track progress and measure the results.

Agreed upon – The goal must be relevant, and all parties must agree on it.

Realistic – The goal meant to be achieved must be realistic and actually doable.

Time bound – The goal has a timeframe and a deadline.

Ethical – The goal is ethical and you feel comfortable doing it.

Resourced – The resources to achieve the goal—time, money, and people—are available to get it done.

Why is it important?

Identifying the project's importance will help solidify why the project is being started.

If you can't come up with a reason why this is important, then maybe you shouldn't be doing it.

What are the critical constraints, if any?

A constraint is a limitation or restriction, like time or money. For example

- The people you need may not be available.

- There is limited money.

- The project must be done by a certain date.

When does it need to be complete? And what is "complete"?

What's the general timeframe for the project? When should it be done? If possible, it's best to use date ranges.

Talk with the sponsor and determine what defines "complete." For example

- Everyone has been trained.

- Everything was produced and delivered.

You want to make sure expectations are clearly defined upfront so the sponsor/customer knows it when they see it. Unexpected revisions along the way can be costly in terms of time, money, and people.

What do you have in mind for a budget?

Whatever you're trying to accomplish may require money. The sponsor usually has some figure in mind for the project. At this stage, any amount will be a high-level guesstimate.

You should update the estimated costs after you've figured out how much work will be involved to get the project done.

The sponsor may ask you for a breakdown of the costs. At this point, this will be your best guess. (This is not something you answer right away but figure out after you've talked with the sponsor/customer and gathered more information about the project.)

Some things to consider when making your guesstimate include the following:

- Internal people cost, e.g. staff

- External people cost, e.g. vendors and contractors

- Non-people cost, e.g. equipment, supplies, and facilities

Don't forget about "on-going costs," the costs you must continually pay *after* the project is complete. These include things like maintenance fees and subscription fees.

Make sure you document how you got your numbers in case someone asks.

What features must be included at the absolute minimum so that the project can still be considered successful?

Answering this question will help you get down to the minimum that the project must include or address in order to still be considered successful.

What things must be produced for the project to be considered successful?

You may need to develop and/or purchase tangible "deliverables" along the way in order for your project to be successful. For instance, if your project is to develop and deliver a training class, a deliverable may be the course outline or training materials.

Talk with the sponsor and determine what must be produced to complete project.

What key events are needed to ensure the project is progressing as planned?

After reviewing the information you've obtained from the sponsor, determine what the key dates, also known as "milestones," are.

Some things to consider include the following:

- When will the project officially start?

- When are you going to have a plan?

- When is each deliverable to be produced?

- When will the results be turned over to whomever asked for them?

- When will the project be finished?

Are you aware of anything that could go wrong? If something does, what should be done about it?

Be aware of things that could go wrong and adversely impact the project: "risks."

Ask, "What could go wrong?" and "If something does, what are we going to do about it?"

Here are some examples of risks:

- Trying new technology

- Key team members being pulled away to work on other things

- Working with a new vendor

- A vendor going out of business

Who can help with the planning?

If you don't know names, identify the roles needed to make the project happen. You want people who are knowledgeable about the subject matter. They are often called "subject matter experts" or "SMEs" for short.

If you don't know who or where they are, ask. And don't assume that just because you want some SMEs you'll get them.

Whomever these people work for will usually want to know whom you need, how many hours you need them per week/day, and for how long. Some of these questions can't be answered until you know more about the work to be performed. For now just try to determine how long you'll need them to help you develop the plan.

Who will be impacted and who has a strong personal interest in the project? What will the impact be and how should we handle it?

Talk with the sponsor/customer and identify the following:

- Who will benefit from the project?

- Who might be negatively impacted by the project?

- Who has a strong personal interest in the project (good or bad)?

These people are called "stakeholders." (Team members are considered stakeholders also.)

Try to identify what impact the project will have on these people. This will help you identify things you may need to plan for, communicate, and manage.

Some things to think about include the following:

- Will people need to be trained?

- Will processes need to be developed, modified, or eliminated?

Who needs to know what's going on with the project?

This has to do with whether or not you need to communicate what you're doing, as well as your progress, to anyone else.

If you are doing something for someone else, such as your boss or a client, then it definitely pays to keep this person informed about what's going on and where things stand.

Things you want to consider include the following:

- Who wants to know?

- Why do they need to know?

- What do they need to know?

- When do they need to know it?

- How often do they need to know it?

- How should the information be shared with them?

A good place to put this information is in a spreadsheet. This can become your communications plan.

Fill in the gaps

After you've met with the sponsor, you may have to track down some information.

And depending on the size and complexity of whatever you're trying to do, you may need to talk to some other people or do some research. Remember, Google is your best friend.

Write up the information

Once you've gathered all the information, you should put it into a nicely formatted document or form, called a "project charter" or "project scope document." This will make it easier for others to read and understand.

You may want to get someone you trust to review it for you.

You want to get this one right

There are two documents that I consider critical to any project. One is the project charter; the other is the plan.

The project charter defines what you're going to do; the plan defines how you're going to do it.

If you don't remember anything else, remember that. You can basically run your project with just those two things.

Review the information with the sponsor and get approval to continue

It's important to review the project charter with the sponsor. You want to make sure everything is clear and understood *before* you figure out what work is required to do it.

How long will it take to define it?

Well, the answer is, it depends. It will depend on the following:

- The size and complexity of what you're trying to accomplish

- Your experience with doing this type of thing

Once again, use Google to gather information. Or you can work with someone like me to help you figure it out quickly.

Now it's time to figure out what you have to do

Now that you have defined the project, it's time to figure out what it will take to make it happen.

Tips

Talk to other who may have done a project like yours. If you can't find a person who has done this before, brainstorm with someone to come up with reasonable milestones, deliverables, and costs. The focus should be on the big stuff for the moment.

Worksheet – What You Need to Know about the Project Checklist

What You Need to Know about the Project

1. What's the project's goal or outcome?

2. Why is it important?

3. What are the critical resource constraints, if any? (A constraint is a limitation; it usually involves time, money, or people.)

4. When does it need to be complete, and what is considered "complete"?

5. What's the budget?

6. What absolute minimum features must be included for the project to be considered successful?

7. What things need to be created and/or purchased?

8. What are the key events/milestones you expect to see to ensure the project is progressing as expected?

9. Are you aware of anything that could go wrong? And if something does, what should be done about it?

10. Who can help with the plan? Who is a good point of contact for developing the plan?

11. Who will be impacted either positively or negatively by it? What is the impact and how should we deal with it?

12. Who has a strong personal interest in the project?

13. Who needs to know about the project's progress? What do they need to know, why do they need to know, when do they need to know it, how often do they need to know, and how should the information be shared with them?

Worksheet – Project Charter

Project Charter

Project Name:

Project Manager:

Sponsor:

Customer:

Start: Finish:

Budget:

Known Critical Constraints: [ ] Time [ ] Money [ ] People

Reason for the Project : *<Why are we doing this?>*

Project Goal : *< What's the goal of the project? What's the expected outcome?>*

Scope: *<What are the requirements? What absolutely must be included?>*

What's considered done? : *<How will we know when we're done?>*

Key Milestones/Deliverable

Milestone	Deliverable	Due Date

Known Risks

What could go wrong	Chances of it happening	Impact if it does happen	What should be done about it

Team

Role	Name	When needed	For how long

Signature: Date:

Worksheet – Communications Plan

Communications Plan			
Who needs to know			
What do they need to know			
Why do they need to know			
When do they need to know it			
How often do they need to know			
How should the info be shared with them			

Step 2 – Come Up with a Plan to Do It

Planning is an unnatural process; it is much more fun to do something. The nicest thing about not planning is that failure comes as a complete surprise, rather than being preceded by a period of worry and depression.

—*Sir John Harvey-Jones*

What's the plan?

Now that you have the project defined, you need to come up with the work that needs to be done to achieve the goal or outcome.

This involves coming up with the steps or tasks you need to take, who needs to work on each task, when the task needs to get done, and how much money you may need to spend and when.

If you don't define what you have to do, then you'll be flying by the seat of your pants.

What are the benefits of planning?

Defining the work will help you to become clear about what it will take to accomplish what you set out to do. You'll have a step-by-step roadmap to guide you and your team from start to finish.

How long will planning take?

Once again, it will depend on how much you already know about what has to be done and how familiar you are with the subject matter.

What do you have to do to deliver the goods?

Look at your project charter. What deliverables have to be produced? What milestones have to be met?

Your deliverables and milestones are the starting points for coming up with the tasks. You start by further breaking down each one. For each one, ask yourself, "What things must happen to produce this deliverable or hit this date?" Make a list.

If you have trouble trying to break them down, try one of these techniques:

- See if it's been done before.

- Brainstorm.

- Mind map.

See if it's been done before

If you believe what you're doing has been done before somewhere, do the following:

- Ask your colleagues or friends.

- Check out Google. The problem with Google, though, is you may have to wade through a lot of stuff to find something decent.

- Check online forums or other social media and ask if anyone has ever done a project like yours before. Many people are helpful.

Or you can get together your team, a group of co-workers, or some friends to work through it together.

Brainstorm

Brainstorming is a method used to generate ideas. While brainstorming, you don't worry about staying organized. The goal is to pour your thoughts onto paper without worrying about whether they make sense or how they fit together.

For your project, write down everything you can think of that has to be done to get you from the start to the finish. These thoughts should produce the deliverables and milestones. You can use a piece of paper, sticky notes, a white board, or software.

Just jot down each thing that has to be created as well as the major events that need to happen.

Under each, jot down the actions it will take to get it done.

Mind map

Mind mapping is my all-time favorite tool to use when it comes to planning! It's fun, it's easy, and it doesn't take much time to come up with the work to be done.

A mind map is a graphical way to represent words, ideas, actions, or concepts.

To start, take a piece of paper or use a white board; draw a circle in the center. Inside the circle, write the outcome you're trying to achieve.

Next, draw a bubble or circle for each major event and/or each deliverable. Draw a line from the center circle to each bubble.

Next, begin jotting down the things that need to happen to achieve what's in the bubble.

Other things you should probably include

Just producing the deliverables isn't enough. You need to make sure you account for administrative-type things like meetings, reviews, and your time.

Other things you may want to include are:

- Your time to manage the project

- Team meetings

- Review meetings

- Informing others

How long will each task take?

This is where you guesstimate how long it will take to do each step.

Unexpected things occur on any project. You may want to add time either to each task or to the schedule to account for unexpected events. The amount of time will depend on how confident you are that everything has been covered. A good place to start is to add around 10 percent more time.

Who will do the work?

Next, figure out who will do the work. If it's you, that's fine. If you need help, then jot down the skills you need or specifically whom (if you know) you need.

What supplies, equipment, facilities, or other resources do you need?

Depending on what you're doing, you may need to get supplies, equipment, or other things. Looking at each step, you need to determine if you need resources other than people.

If you need to have these resources, you must also determine the cost of each.

Schedule Out the Work

Sequence the tasks

After you have come up with the steps involved in what needs to be created and the events that need to happen, then it's time to take a look at them and decide what should come first, second, third, and so on.

Working with the team, you need to put the tasks into a logical sequence. The task list should contain the estimated hours and resources needed for each task. Sticky notes work well for this.

Some things to consider include the following:

• Which tasks can be performed at the same time?

• Which tasks are dependent on other tasks? (These are called "dependencies"; they must occur before something else can happen.)

Calculate the start and end dates

Using the time estimates, calculate the start and end date for each task.

There is a difference between time and duration. "Time" is how many hours it will take to get the work done, whereas "duration" is the length of time it will take you to get it done.

Let's say that the task requires four hours to complete. The person assigned has only one hour a day to spend on it. Therefore, the time it takes to get the task done will be four hours, but the duration will be four days or more.

Review how much time each person is working

Review the hours per week or day for each person to make sure individuals aren't overloaded. Ensure they aren't working more hours than are available for them to work. If they are, adjust the schedule by either stretching out the task or assigning a different person, if you can.

When will the project be done?

Drum roll, please! Now that you've laid out your plan and you have dates, you know when the project will be finished.

Is this end date anywhere close to what you thought it would be when you defined the project? If not, there's hope.

Is each step essential?

Look over your schedule and determine if everything on it actually needs to get done. Is it essential or just nice to have?

Can you get more people?

See if you can get more help to complete the project.

What's it really going to cost?

Look at all the stuff you need to buy and all the people you may need, and ask yourself, "What's it really going to cost to do this?" Is it anywhere close to what you thought? Do you have the funds to cover it, or is it way more than what the budget calls for?

If you are paying contractors, consultants, or vendors or if you are pur-
chasing something, then it's probably a good idea to track what you're
spending. You should also figure out how much you'll be spending per
week, month, or quarter (whichever period works best for you and your
organization).

If it's going to cost at least 10% or more than the budget, you may want
to consider cutting out some things especially if controlling the costs is
important to the sponsor/customer.

You can also consider looking into cheaper resources: people, equipment, etc.
The downside of this is you may just get what you pay for. Buyer be warned!

Review the schedule with the planning team

Once you have pulled the schedule together, review the schedule with the
planning team to see if it seems reasonable. Make any necessary adjustments.

Look at your project charter. How do the deliverables and milestone dates
compare? Are they close or really far apart?

**Review the milestones and costs with the sponsor if they are very
different from what they are in the project charter**

Review the major project milestones and budget with the sponsor to make
sure he or she agrees with the proposed dates.

If the sponsor isn't happy with the dates or costs, you may be asked to make
further adjustments.

How can you make the process easier?

To make things easier for you, I've included a worksheet at the end of
the chapter. Or you can develop your own using a spreadsheet or project

management software. If you're interested in learning more about software, check out the "Leveraging Technology" section.

Tips

To make this process more efficient, gather the planning team in a room and use sticky notes and markers, or just use a white board.

Use the sticky notes to jot down what has to be done and then post them on a wall. This approach makes it easy to move things around.

Alternatively, you can use mind-mapping software or a white board to draw out the high-level tasks and sub-tasks. Free mind-mapping software is available on the Internet.

Worksheet – Map out the Work

Worksheet – Project Plan

Project Plan					
#	Milestone/Task	Assigned To	Start	End	Status

Worksheet – Money Tracker

People Costs	Amt. Budgeted	Amt. Spent <xx/xx/xx>	Amt. Spent <xx/xx/xx>	Total Spent	Remaining
<person's name or vendor name>	*<dollar amount>*	*<dollar amount>*	*<dollar amount>*	*<dollar amount>*	*<dollar amount>*
Non-People Costs	**Amt. Budgeted**	**Amt. Spent**<xx/xx/xx>	**Amt. Spent** <xx/xx/xx>	**Total Spent**	**Remaining**
<things including equipment, supplies, and facilities>	*<dollar amount>*	*<dollar amount>*	*<dollar amount>*	*<dollar amount>*	*<dollar amount>*
Totals	*<dollar amount>*	*<dollar amount>*	*<dollar amount>*	*<dollar amount>*	*<dollar amount>*

Work the Plan

The truth of the matter is that you always know the right thing to do. The hard part is doing it.

—General H. Norman Schwarzkopf

Step 3 – Get Everyone Focused

If everyone is moving forward together, then success takes care of itself.

—Henry Ford

Time to get everyone on the same page

Projects work best if all the players are on the same page. One way to do that is to hold a kick-off meeting.

Doing so allows everyone to find out what the project is about; to review the work that has to be done; and to learn each person's roles, responsibilities, and expectations. The meeting also gives everyone a chance to ask questions.

Set an agenda

Set an agenda for the kick-off meeting and include the following:

- A review of the project plan including schedule, staffing, and budget

- A review of the roles, responsibilities, and expectations

- A progress meeting schedule and attendance expectations

- A reporting schedule and expectations

- How problems and changes will be handled

- A Q&A

- The date of the first progress meeting

Schedule the meeting

Schedule the meeting and invite the project team, sponsor, and other key people. Include a copy of the agenda with the invite.

Hold the meeting

Make sure you have an agenda, a copy of the project charter, and a copy of the plan for everyone.

In addition, be sure to communicate the date of the first review meeting so that people can get it on their calendars.

Capture any decisions, issues, or action items that come up during the discussion.

Distribute the meeting minutes

Write up and send out meeting minutes to participants and invitees in a timely fashion.

Now, let the work begin!

Time to get to it!

Tips

Make sure you schedule the meeting well enough in advance because calendars tend to fill up and everyone is busy.

Worksheet – Kick-off Meeting Agenda

Kick-off Meeting Agenda	
Project Name:	
Meeting Date:	
Facilitator:	
Invited:	
Attendees:	

Agenda		
Agenda Item	**Presenter**	**Time**
Introduce the team.		
Review the project charter.		
Review the work plan.		
Review the roles, responsibilities, and expectations.		
Review the meeting schedule and expectations.		
Review the reporting schedule and expectations.		
Review how problems and changes will be handled.		
Hold a Q&A.		

Action Items for Follow-up		
Action Item	Assigned To	Date Due

Step 4 – Make Sure the Work Gets Done

A project gets a year late one day at a time.

—Unknown

Just get it done

This step is about ensuring the work is moving along as planned. You may be doing the work yourself, or perhaps others are doing the work with you. Either way, it needs to get done.

If you don't ensure things are progressing, you won't accomplish what you set out to do in the first place. (If the work isn't completed, you'd better have documentation to back yourself up since you will not have achieved the outcome of the project!)

Nothing feels better than finishing what you set out to do. And nothing is more frustrating than feeling as if you have wasted a lot of time and energy—and, potentially, money—and nothing came of it.

Your daily/weekly review process

One of the best ways to keep things on track is to have a daily or weekly review process. (A checklist works really well for this.)

Prepare for the review

First, gather all the information you're going to review:

- The plan

- The problem/change/action item–tracking document

- The money-tracking document

If you have a team, you may want to do the following:

- Schedule a face-to-face or virtual review meeting.

- Prepare an agenda to cover reviewing the plan, any open and new items, and any upcoming absences.

- Send the agenda to the team with a reminder to be prepared to discuss anything that is assigned to each team member, plus any new items.

- Hold the meeting.

What to review

Simple enough. Here, you review what was supposed to be achieved and check off if these tasks were done or not.

If you are managing the work and someone else is doing it, you need to find out from that person if the work is complete or not.

A word of caution! Don't buy into "percent complete"! What is that, you ask? Well, here's how that goes:

You: "Is the task done?"

Them: "No."

You: "Where are you on it?"

Them: "Oh, I'm about 50 percent complete."

You: "Okay."

NO! What the heck does "50 percent complete" mean? In my experience, it means absolutely NOTHING!

Instead, you should be asking what exactly has been done, what specifically remains to be done, and how long it is going to take until it is done.

These concrete questions will give you a better picture as to the person's true progress.

Which things aren't being completed on time or are not starting when they should?

If the work isn't starting or finishing on time, other things may slip as well.

Find out which tasks are behind. Review the schedule and mark any task whose end date has passed.

Find out which tasks haven't started but should have. Review the schedule and mark any task whose start date has passed.

Look at the tasks that are late or behind. Are other tasks waiting for them to end before they start? If other tasks are waiting on the late tasks, your schedule may slip. You may need to adjust the schedule or assignments to keep the plan on track.

Talk to the people assigned to the tasks that are late or behind and find out what is going on, so that you can address the problem. Make sure you know why these individuals are late or behind.

Here are some questions to consider asking so you can make up for lost time:

- What people are needed to put the plan back on track or to accelerate it?

- Can the work be assigned to someone else?

- Can someone else be added to the task?

- Can the duration be shortened?

- Can the work be combined with another task?

Adjust task dates, assignments, and durations.

Review the schedule to see if you can adjust anything else.

Review the remaining schedule to ensure lead times and so on are still okay. Make any necessary adjustments.

After you've made all the adjustments, see if the end date has shifted significantly. If you are not going to make your end date, you need to let the sponsor know.

What's coming up next week?

Look at the schedule and see what tasks are coming up for the next week so you and your team can get prepared.

Where do you stand on the open items that are now due?

Look at the other items that have been assigned (such as problems, changes, and action items) and ascertain if progress has been made on them. If not, ask, "Why not?" and "What needs to be done to get them closed?"

Have any new items come up?

Have any new problems or changes popped since your last review? If so, what are they? If you have a team, make sure you assign the new items so that they can be handled.

Are there any other challenges?

This is to address anything that was not covered by the other questions.

Where are you on the money?

Managing the costs is all about understanding how the financial situation is shaping up. If you know all about the money, you can understand if you are where you should be based on where you are in the project.

You should be keeping track of how much money you have spent so far and how much you have left.

If you are dealing with external people (such as contractors, consultants, and vendors) and/or are making purchases, make sure you know the cost of what was requested and how much you are being billed. Doing so will allow you to keep good records.

If you don't have access to this information, you may wish to work with your organization's accounting or finance people to get it (if they exist in your organization).

Keep track of this information on a spreadsheet or a ledger. If you use a spreadsheet, you can set it up to do the calculations automatically. This way, you can see how much money you have left (if any).

Make adjustments as necessary to reflect any changes in the costs. Make sure these changes have been *approved*. *(See Step 6 – Deal with any changes.)*

If what has been spent is more than the budget, or well below it, make sure you know why and be prepared to explain the discrepancy.

Consider the following:

• If what has been spent so far is well below the budget, the project may be behind schedule.

• If what has been spent so far is well over what you had intended to spend at this point in time, the project may be spending money faster than you expected, which could leave you short on money at the end.

Based on where you are right now on the schedule, you need to determine if you'll have enough money to finish the project.

Make sure you document the differences, what caused them, and what you're going to do about them in the future. This information will be of interest to whoever is paying for the project.

After the review

Capture and update anything that needs to be updated.

If you have a team, send team members a copy of the updated information and let them know the date of the next review meeting.

Tips

Make sure you know where things stand at all times.

Worksheet – Project Review Checklist

Project Review Checklist

☐ Review the work plan.

- What has been completed since the last review?

- What didn't finish that should have finished?

- What didn't start that should have started?

- What's coming up in the next day/week?

- Do you have enough people to finish?

- What's the projected end date?

☐ Review the problems/changes.

- What items have been closed since the last review?

- What's the status of the open items?

- If the item is past due, what is being done about it?

- What items are coming due?

- Are there any new items?

- Are there other challenges that need to be addressed?

☐ Review the money.

- How much has been spent since the last review?

- Are there outstanding or overdue bills? How much is owed on them?

- How much money is remaining?

- How much money do you need to finish?

Worksheet – Project Team Meeting Agenda

Project Team Meeting Agenda	
Project Name:	
Meeting Date:	
Facilitator:	
Invited:	
Attendees:	

Agenda	
Agenda Item	**Time**
Review the project plan.	
Discuss what's coming up before the next review.	
Review and discuss open problems, changes, and action items.	
Discuss any new problems, changes, and/or concerns.	
Discuss upcoming meetings.	
Discuss upcoming absences.	
Hold a Q&A.	

Decisions		
Decision Made	**Impact**	**Action Required**

New Problems/Changes		
Problem/Change	**Assigned To**	**Date Due**

Action Items for Follow-up		
Action Item	**Assigned To**	**Date Due**

Step 5 – Handle the Problems

The problem is not that there are problems. The problem is expecting otherwise and thinking that having problems is a problem.

—Theodore Rubin

Things happen

Problems pop up and need to be dealt with. When they show their ugly little faces, make sure you make note of each problem and assess its impact on your plan. Then work to fix it.

If you are doing the project for someone else, make sure you let that person know of any open problems, what their impact could be, and what you plan to do about the problems and when.

If someone is doing the work for you, make sure you specifically ask if there are any problems. You need to know and understand the impact and find out what and when something will be done about it.

Sponsors/customers hate surprises. And if you're not careful, these "little" problems can derail your plan.

Track the problems

Problems that are not properly managed may adversely affect the plan, the money, and the people. The key to avoiding this situation is to make sure problems are captured, assigned to someone to resolve, and tracked.

Information you should capture includes the following:

- What the problem is

- What the impact will be if the problem is not resolved

- When it was discovered

- Who is assigned to resolve it

- By when it needs to be resolved

- What the actual resolution is

Review the problems daily/weekly as part of your review process

Problems should be reviewed as part of your review process. As new problems arise throughout the week, you need to add them to the list. Problems that have been resolved should be updated on the tracking spreadsheet to indicate how they were resolved.

For problems that still need to be addressed, get the current status by talking with the person assigned to take care of it. Update the information.

You may need to have a process for how to handle problems that can't be resolved within the team; this is called an "escalation process." This will help to ensure problems don't just linger without ever being resolved.

Tips

Give the project team members access to the item-tracking spreadsheet and encourage them to use it.

Worksheet – Item Tracker

Date Entered	Issue/Change/Action	Assigned To	Priority (H, M, L)	Status (Open, Closed)	Due Date	Impact (Scope, Schedule, Budget)	Date Closed

Step 6 – Deal with Any Changes

There is nothing wrong with change, if it is in the right direction.

—*Winston Churchill*

The only constant is change

It goes without saying that things will change. Changes that slip in under the radar can quickly derail a project. The results could be disastrous for you and the project. Dates could slip, costs might go crazy, and you could end up not delivering the outcome that was expected. Therefore, to keep your schedule and costs in check, you must deal with the changes.

Track the changes

Changes—such as changes in costs, schedule, or resources—should be captured and the impact of them identified and quantified, so that an informed decision can be made about whether or not to make the change. *No change should be made without having the change documented and approved.*

Information you should capture includes the following:

- What the nature of the change is

- How the costs , the schedule, and the resources will be impacted

- What the value of making the change is

- What the cost of the change is (analyze, for example, how much time needs to be added to the schedule, how much it will cost, and how many hours it will take to make the change)

Review the changes daily/weekly as part of your review process

Changes should be reviewed at the weekly progress meeting. As new changes arise throughout the week, you and/or your team members should add the new ones to the list.

Talk with the person who submitted the change and make sure you understand exactly what the change is about, why it's needed, and what the potential impact is.

Review the changes with the sponsor/customer

Changes that will cause the project to end late, cost more money, or affect the goal should be reviewed and approved and/or rejected by the sponsor/customer *before* any work is done.

Tips

Make sure the sponsor/customer is aware of and participates in the change review process. In addition, stress to the team that *no changes* are to be made until they have been approved.

Worksheet – Item Tracker

Date Entered	Issue/Change/Action	Assigned To	Priority (H, M, L)	Status (Open, Closed)	Due Date	Impact (Scope, Schedule, Budget)	Date Closed

Step 7 – Manage the Team

We're a team. One person struggles, we all struggle. One person triumphs, we all triumph.

—Unknown

It's about leadership

In addition to managing your project, you may have a team to manage. Managing teams is all about leadership.

What is a leader?

A leader is the person who guides or directs the group. He or she is accountable and responsible to the group, sets the vision, and inspires and enables them to achieve results. The leader also accepts full responsibility for failure.

What your team should expect from you

- Keep things on track.

- Have regular progress meetings.

- Hold effective and efficient meetings.

- Communicate any issues or changes in a timely manner.

- Attend project meetings as required; communicate to the team when it is not possible to attend.

- Take the responsibility to review any session information that was missed prior to the next session.

- Freely pass along information that might be useful to team members.

- Offer to help when others are busy or running behind.

- Work to ensure information is clear, concise, and understandable.

- Keep the interest of team members in mind whenever it is appropriate.

- Listen attentively, and genuinely seek to understand others' viewpoints.

- Work with team members to resolve conflicts when they arise within the team.

- Welcome suggestions for improvements.

What you should expect from your team

Skills and experience

Team members should be expected to contribute their skills and experience to the project to help ensure its successful completion.

Planning

To the extent possible, team members should plan the required work within their area of expertise to ensure that schedule and budget expectations are reasonable.

Authority

Team members should have the authority to make decisions and act within the scope of their role on the project.

Communication

Team members should maintain open communications with you so that the project may stay on schedule and issues may be handled in a timely manner.

Commitment

Team members should allocate the necessary time required to get the project work done and be available to assist others, if necessary, to keep the project on schedule.

Participation

Team members should actively participate in the project planning and review meetings and need to look for opportunities to share information and assist other project team members.

Reporting

Team members should update you on their task status on a frequency dictated by you, and they should ensure that the information is concise, relevant, and clear.

Tips

Clearly define and communicate the expectations, roles, and responsibilities to the team.

Step 8 – Keep Everyone Informed

Communication is the real work of leadership.

—*Nitin Nohria*

Project management is 90 percent communication

Real estate is location, location, location. For projects, it is communication, communication, communication. The more you keep people informed, the better off you'll be.

People like to know what's going on with anything that's going to impact them either positively or negatively or that they are paying for.

Ongoing communication should be part of your overall schedule, but project managers often fail to add it.

Develop a communications plan if you need one but don't have one

If you haven't already done so, you may need to develop a communications plan. You should have identified this information when you were defining the project.

You want to keep the team, the sponsor, your boss, the stakeholders, and the customers/users informed of where things stand in the project.

How to communicate

Look at your communications plan. Different groups and individuals may require different kinds of communications. Some people just need to be aware, whereas others will want all the gory details of what's going on. Most people impacted by a project will want to know what's in it for them as well as when and how they will be impacted.

How often you communicate will depend on how and when people will be impacted as well as who they are.

The easiest way to keep track of the communication is to add it to the project schedule.

Handle questions as they come up

As soon as you get questions and feedback, start keeping track of these communications.

If you've fielded questions or concerns, make sure you follow up with an e-mail to respond to whoever is raising the issue or to let the individual know you're looking into it.

Write status reports

A status report gives a snapshot of what's going on with your project. It highlights key accomplishments, where you are on your schedule and costs, and any items that need leadership attention.

Write the status report after you've updated your project information: plan, items, etc. That way, your report will contain the most current information.

Review the previous status report to make sure you're not repeating yourself (unless you intend to repeat yourself).

You need to determine how often you will be reporting on the project's status. If the project is relatively short (and "short" is relative), you should probably do it weekly. Every other week would be a good middle ground. Reserve monthly reporting for projects that are very long, i.e. a year.

As for formatting, practically speaking, the easiest thing to do is write up a summary of the accomplishments, where you stand on the schedule, and what the budget is; summarize your outstanding changes and problems.

What has been accomplished?

Highlight significant accomplishments made since the last reporting period.

Make sure that the accomplishments contain no jargon, that acronyms (such as FBI) are spelled out before being used, and that the language is audience appropriate.

Where do you stand on the milestones and deliverables?

List all the key dates with their planned end dates and actual completion dates.

Some things to consider include the following:

- If key dates are past due, be prepared to explain why and what's being done about it.

- If the dates aren't being met, the results may not be delivered when expected.

Where do you stand on the money?

List how much money you started with, how much you've spent so far, how much is remaining, and how much more you think you'll need if what's remaining isn't enough.

Some things to consider include the following:

- If you don't have enough money left to finish the project, then you may be spending faster than you thought or more than you thought.

- If you are spending too slowly, things are running behind, you didn't estimate the costs properly, you're not getting the bills from your vendors in a timely manner, or you're not paying the bills in a timely manner.

Where do you stand on the problems?

List all the open problems that will impact the project, along with their descriptions and due dates.

Some things to consider include the following:

- If the due date is past due, be prepared to explain why and what's being done to address it.

- If the due date is past due, that means you haven't done anything to resolve it or you need help to get it resolved.

Where do you stand on the changes?

List all the proposed changes that will impact the project, along with their descriptions. Be prepared to explain the impact in terms of time, money, and people.

Review it before sending it out

Read through the status report to ensure that it makes sense, that there are no misspellings, and that the language fits the audience.

Send it out

Distribute the status report to everyone who needs to know what's going on with the project.

Tips

Since about 90 percent of what you will be doing is communicating, make sure to stay on top of the communications. Team members shouldn't have to come to you and ask what's going on. You should be proactive in letting them know.

Worksheet – Project Status Report

Project Status Report for Period Ending ___/___/___

Project Name:	
Project Manager:	

Project Status Summary: Green Yellow Red

Key Accomplishments since Last Period:

List brief descriptions (one or two sentences) of what was accomplished in this last period:

☐ Accomplishment 1

☐ Accomplishment 2

Key Milestones/Deliverables

Milestone/Deliverable	Planned	Actual	Status
Explanation:			

Issues/Changes Requiring Management Attention:

Issue/Change	Priority	Due
Explanation:		

Budget

Budget	Total Spent So Far	Amt Remaining	Amt Needed to Finish
Explanation:			

Close It Out

Do not plan for ventures before finishing what's at hand.

—Euripides

Step 9 – Wrap It Up

"Begin at the beginning," the King said gravely, "and go on till you come to the end; then stop."

—Lewis Carroll, *Alice in Wonderland*

It's not over 'til it's over

If all the work is done, then you're almost "done done." "Almost" means that there are still a few things to do before you close this puppy down.

If everything is "done done," then you've wrapped everything up with a neat little bow and turned it over to whoever asked for it in the first place.

Hold a final project review meeting with the team

Meet with the team to review the plan, items, and costs.

Is all the work done?

Review the plan and make sure that everything that was supposed to be complete is.

Are there any outstanding items that need to be addressed?

Review the item tracking sheets to determine how any open items will be handled. Outstanding problems may have to be fixed before the project is considered "done."

Are there any outstanding bills?

Find out from the team if anyone has ordered anything or received anything that perhaps you hadn't heard about before.

Some things to consider include the following:

- Find out what was ordered and received, when it was ordered and/or received, who supplied it, and how much it cost. *(No one should have ordered anything unless you knew about it!)*

- Gather any invoices that team members may have but that they forgot to mention to you.

What are the lessons learned?

Find out from your team what went well, what didn't go so well, and what could be done differently in the future. Take notes and save them for your next project.

Is everything paid?

Some outstanding invoices may still be lingering. You need to review your costs and make sure you have accounted for everything.

If there are outstanding invoices, find out what they are for and how much is owed. This could make or break your costs estimates. Usually, you don't want to close out the accounting numbers until everything has been paid.

Check with your vendors (if you used them)

Call your vendors and find out if you have received all the invoices. If you haven't, find out which ones are missing, how much they are for, and when you can expect receive to them.

Document the outstanding costs

Make sure you write down what the outstanding bills are and when you expect to receive them. Total up the bill amounts.

Check your money-tracking spreadsheet to see if money is available to cover the expenses

Compare the costs remaining to the total outstanding bill amounts.

Some things to consider include the following:

- Whether you do or you don't have enough money, the bills have to be paid. You need to be concerned about whether paying these bills will push you over your budget; if so, you need to know by how much and where the money to cover the bills will come from.

- If you're going to go over, make sure no one is going to have a cow about it. If someone is upset about it, you need to work with your sponsor or finance folks to figure out how the costs will be covered. The money has already been spent. Someone has to pay for it.

Prepare a final status report

Before writing your final report, make sure you're aware of any outstanding problems that people may be experiencing and ensure the team is working to resolve them.

If you have time, talk to the customers personally so that you are aware of what's going on. You want the meeting to be as favorable as possible.

Write a final project status that reflects the following:

- The results that were delivered

- All the key dates and when they were actually completed

- Any outstanding problems or changes

- The final costs (be prepared to explain if you spent more than expected)

Walk through the final status report with the sponsor/customer

Now it's time for the sponsor/customer to review what got delivered and to make sure there are no major issues.

From the sponsor/customer's perspective (usually), the project is done once everything has been delivered, even though there are a few things remaining to do before the project can really be called "done."

The meeting should be held at least a week or two after everything's complete.

Be prepared to discuss and/or defend any schedule or costs overrun. Know how much money may be outstanding. (This may occur if you have outstanding invoices.)

Release the team

By this time, the team members have usually already started working on other things. If not, it's time to release them and let whoever they work for know that the project is over.

Tips

Don't skip this step. It's important to bring everything to a close.

Worksheet – What Did We Learn?

What Did We Learn?

There are no mistakes or failures, only lessons.

—Denis Waitley

Steps	+/-	Notes
Define what you're trying to do.		
Come up with a plan to do it.		
Get everyone focused.		
Make sure the work gets done.		
Handle the problems.		
Deal with any changes.		
Manage the team.		
Keep everyone informed.		
Wrap it up.		
Celebrate.		

Review each step and quickly assess if things went well (+) or if there were challenges (-). Add any notes about what you and/or the team believe should be done differently next time to make things faster and smoother and to ensure nothing slips through the cracks.

Worksheet – Are We Done Checklist

Are We Done Checklist

☐ Has a final meeting been held with the team?

☐ Have lessons learned been documented and distributed?

☐ Are all the tasks complete?

☐ Have all the deliverables been completed and signed off as appropriate?

☐ Has everything been delivered to the customer?

☐ Have all the outstanding invoices been gathered?

☐ Have all the outstanding costs been documented?

☐ Have all the outstanding problems and changes been identified?

☐ Has the final status report been created?

☐ Has the final review meeting with the sponsor/customer been held?

☐ Has the project been closed with your accounting and/or finance group?

☐ Have team members been released?

☐ Has a date been set for the project celebration?

☐ Is the Project File complete?

☐ Has the complete Project File been archived?

NOTES:

Step 10 – Celebrate

No one succeeds alone.

—Unknown

It's over!

You finally made it, and you're done. It is hoped that the sponsor and customers are satisfied. (That remains to be seen.)

Anyway, it may be time for you and the project team members to move on to other tasks and assignments.

But before everyone scatters to the four winds, it's nice to acknowledge all the hard work and to thank the team members for their contributions. It also makes them feel as if someone actually appreciated what they accomplished.

Talk to the sponsor about having some type of celebration

Talk to the sponsor about pitching in for a celebration. Jot down the names of everyone who was involved in the project and what role they played.

Some things to consider include the following:

- Should everyone outside the project team be included?

- How much money is available?

- If the sponsor can't or won't fund it, are you willing to hold a celebration for the team anyway?

Determine what type of event you want to have

Ask the project team members what type of event would work for them. What you end up doing largely depends on how big the project was and what type of funding is available.

Some things to consider include the following:

- Breakfast – start the day off with a celebration.

- Late lunch with the rest of the day off – people usually like this because it gives them time to enjoy themselves without worrying about coming back to work. In addition, it doesn't interfere with their home life, such as picking up kids.

- Dinner – dinner may be challenging as it may interfere with home life.

- Drinks after work – some people like this, some don't.

- Potluck – everyone brings something. This may work if you have limited funds but still want to celebrate with the team. Some people enjoy showing off their cooking skills.

- Team outing – perhaps the group would like to go bowling. See what they would be interested in doing.

- Special events – baseball games, football games, etc.

- Gift certificates.

- Schedule the event.

- Try to plan a time that works for most folks. Not everyone may be able to attend.

Prepare for the event

Treat the event like a micro project:

- Make reservations.

- Send out invitations.

- If you are ordering a small gift for each team member, order the gifts.

- If you are giving award certificates, get them designed and printed.

- Confirm the invites.

- Confirm the reservation.

Hold the event

Get everyone together and have fun!

Some things to consider include the following:

- Say a few words of thanks to the team.

- If the sponsor/customer is there, invite him or her to say a few words as well.

Have fun!

Make sure you thank everyone for a job well done and have fun!

Tips

Enjoy yourself!

Worksheet – Let's Celebrate Checklist

Let's Celebrate Checklist

☐ Talk to your boss, sponsor, or customer about having an event.

☐ Gather the name of everyone who participated on the project.

☐ Determine the type of event you wish to have.

☐ Determine the amount of money that will be needed.

☐ Get approval to hold the event.

☐ Schedule the event.

☐ Send invitations out to everyone who participated on the project.

☐ Prepare for the event.

☐ Hold the event.

☐ Thank everyone!

☐ Have fun!

NOTES:

Set Yourself Up for Success

Men never plan to be failures; they simply fail to plan to be successful.

—William A. Ward

Manage Your Time

You will never find time for anything. If you want time you must make it.

—*Charles Buxton*

What is time management?

Time management is the act or process of planning and exercising control over the amount of time you spend on specific activities. It is a necessity in managing projects as it helps you to achieve the goal or outcome in the specified timeframe.

Where is your time going?

If you're really good at managing your time, then great! You can skip this section.

If, however, you find yourself overwhelmed and stressed out by the thought of adding one more thing to your plate, then read on.

Time robbers

Time robbers steal valuable time away from you. In some cases, other people are robbing you of time. You may or may not have total control over these particular time robbers.

Other time robbers are self-inflicted. In other words, you rob yourself of time. Most of these are under your total control.

Imposed by others

Interruptions

These include things like phone calls or people dropping by to chat.

Waiting for answers

This is the time spent waiting for someone else to get back to you about something.

Unnecessary meetings

This is one of my pet peeves! Many of us spend hours and hours each day in meetings. Many of these meetings are too long or unnecessary.

Too much work

You simply have too much going on at once.

Red tape

This is another of my pet peeves. These are all the policies, procedures, systems, and other hoops that you must jump through to get certain things done.

Self-inflicted

Procrastination

This is the most common time robber: putting things off until later.

Being disorganized

The more disorganized you are, the more time it will take to get anything done.

Absentmindedness

Forgetfulness can result in lost time.

Socializing

You can lose a lot of time if you stop to chat with everyone or if you have to deal with people popping by to talk to you.

Fatigue

If you're tired, it's hard to be as productive as you could be.

Lack of self-discipline

You know what you need to do, but you have a hard time getting it done.

Poor planning

Trying to pull things together without any plan can be time consuming.

Perfectionism

You spend a lot of time trying to make things perfect.

How to manage your time better

Focus on the important things first

What's important, I suppose, is in the eye of the beholder—or something like that.

If you're doing the project within your organization and it's for someone in your organization, then ask what the priority is. If you report to someone, then discuss with that person everything that is on your plate and negotiate the priority of the work you have to do.

Focus on one thing at a time

If at all possible, focus on one project at a time until it's done. While that may not be possible to do all the time, what you can do is focus on dedicating time throughout your day on a specific project without (if possible) interruptions or distractions.

Time box

Time boxing is simply working on a particular task for a specific amount of time. It doesn't have to be finished within the time allotted. It just has to be started and worked on during that time period.

You can put a huge dent in the tasks you need to get done by using an egg timer (or the timer on your cell phone or computer) and by minimizing interruptions and distractions.

Just say, "No!"

This is easier said than done, but sometimes you just have to say no to requests for your time. If the request is coming from management, find out how important the new request is compared to what you're currently working on. Rather than assuming everything is important (which it's not), let management tell you which task is more important.

Tips

Examine where your time is going and come up with a few simple ways to manage it.

Worksheet – Where Does Your Time Go?

Where Does Your Time Go?					
Time Period	Task	Urgent? (Y/N)	Important? (Y/N)	Value (H,M,L)	Time Spent

Leverage Technology

The number one benefit of information technology is that it empowers people to do what they want to do. It lets people be creative. It lets people be productive. It lets people learn things they didn't think they could learn before, and so in a sense it is all about potential.

—Steve Ballmer

How technology can help you

I have to say I'm a techno-geek at heart. I love technology!

I don't like technology just for technology's sake. I like it because of what it allows me to do: streamline and automate tasks and processes. And because of that, I exploit technology for everything its worth! It can help you to do the same.

Simple tools that can help you manage your projects

Pencil and paper

Believe or not, pencil and paper are technology; they're just not automated.

It's really easy just to pull out a few sheets of paper and begin writing. You can define your project; write out your plan; and create templates, draw pictures, and create mind maps. The limit is your imagination.

I do it all the time. I sometimes find it is much easier just to jot things down in a notebook than it is to type them up.

The advantages of pencil and paper are that it's very cheap and easy to use and it's something you're already familiar with.

The disadvantage is that it's not automated and very difficult to share if you need to do that.

Tool suites

Four tool suites come to mind: Google Docs, Microsoft Office for PCs, iWork for Macs, and Open Office.

The nice thing about all of these is they come with software to create the following:

- Spreadsheets

- Documents

- Presentations

- Databases (except Google Docs and iWork)

You may already be using one or more of these, which is great. There's no need to purchase something else unless you just really don't like it.

Google Docs and Open Office are free; Microsoft Office and iWork are not. My personal preference is Microsoft Office, but my husband swears by Open Office. If you don't currently use anything, you might want to try one of the free suites to start.

The advantage to using a suite is that everything within the suite is usually compatible with the other parts of the program. For example, you can build a spreadsheet and embed it into a document or presentation.

The disadvantages of a suite are the expense if you choose to buy one and perhaps the learning curve if the suite is completely new to you. I think they all have a learning curve to one degree or another.

Mind mapping software

As I mentioned before, I'm a huge fan of mind mapping. I use it to jot down thoughts, ideas, and tasks. Mind mapping works similarly to the way I actually think.

The nice thing about mind mapping is you can start with a template and then it becomes fill-in-the-blanks. Simple! I love simple!

Mind maps can help you plan and manage your projects; organize information; brainstorm ideas; plan the writing of reports, documents, or blogs; design a website, book, or publication; or organize your personal tasks. The possibilities are endless.

Software—some of it free—is available online. Search on Google for "best free mind mapping software"; you'll find a wealth of sites to try.

My personal favorite is Mindmanager, which is a paid tool. It runs on my desktop and interfaces with Microsoft Office, which I like.

Mindmanager allows you to develop and run presentations, build websites, and export to a word processor, which is a good starting point when you want to write a document. Mindmanager also offers an online version (I believe for free), but its functionality is limited.

Project management software

If your project is relatively small or medium sized, a spreadsheet may work just fine. You can find worksheets throughout this book as well as on my website. Many organizations use spreadsheets to aid in managing and tracking their projects.

Project management software, like everything else, comes in various flavors. The place to start is what you plan to do with it.

If the project is for you and you really don't need to share the information, then a spreadsheet may work just fine.

If you plan to share the information and collaborate as well as perhaps collect status and keep your clients and boss easily informed, you may want to consider one of the online solutions. (And there are many!)

Or your organization may already have desktop or online tools like Microsoft Project. (Project isn't the easiest tool to use, so beware.)

Many desktop or online tools offer trial versions that allow you to check them out.

Software online is typically known as "software-as-a-service" (SaaS). The difference between SaaS and desktop software is that for SaaS, you pay a subscription fee every month or every year to get access to the software online. With desktop software, on the other hand, you just pay a one-time fee to purchase the software.

How to choose

What do you already have?

Look at the tools you already have and start using them. You're already familiar with these tools, which will make getting started that much faster and easier.

You can develop templates and such as you go or after the project is done.

The cloud or not the cloud? That is the question

What is the "cloud"? The cloud lets you use and store files and applications over the Internet.

These days, it seems that almost everything is moving to the "cloud," and I'm sure that's okay. However, there's a price to be paid for going there: your security and privacy.

How secure is your information? How often is it backed up? What happens if the company servicing you goes belly up? What happens to your stuff?

I'm an online PC gamer, and I've had my account hacked; I've also had my website hijacked, so I personally am just a bit leery of putting EVERYTHING out there. I want to have as much control as possible over my data and information.

So think about it before you go rushing off to put all your stuff, your data, your information, and your projects out on the web.

Tips

Use technology you are comfortable with to reduce the stress and frustration of having to learn something new.

Get Support

When you're drowning, you don't say, 'I would be incredibly pleased if someone would have the foresight to notice me drowning and come and help me,' you just scream.

—*John Lennon*

You don't need to do it alone

Getting support is about being able to ask someone questions, to bounce things off of, and to receive feedback and guidance as you work through your project.

Why you may need support

If this is going to be your first project or you just don't feel comfortable working through it, you may need some help and support.

In my experience, people just starting out need to talk to someone and ask questions. When I set up project management training classes for large corporations, the one thing I stress is the need to provide ongoing support to the newly trained.

Traditional project management training classes are heavy on theory and short on application, so people struggle with how to apply what they have learned. Many come out excited with their newfound skills but quickly get overwhelmed and frustrated when they start. Project management can quickly become a four-letter word.

If you need advice or guidance, and you don't get it, you'll quickly become frustrated. Something that is fairly simple and straightforward will seem painfully difficult and daunting.

Most of us want to do well and succeed in whatever we undertake. Nothing's worse than being tossed into the deep end of the pool without knowing how to swim and without a lifeguard who can jump in and save you when necessary.

What you can do

Take a workshop or class

One way to get help is to take a workshop or class. It's even better if you are allowed to bring your own project to work on. You'll get more out of it.

Get a PM mentor or coach

There are two types of mentors/coaches: free and paid.

Free Mentoring/Coaching

If you happen to know someone—a friend or colleague—who is an experienced project manager (I mean one who knows how to do things the right way), then ask this person if he or she would be willing to answer your questions, provide you with guidance, or review things for you if you need it.

Some organizations have what's called a project management office (PMO). One of their services (usually) is to provide support and guidance to the organization's project managers.

My experience has shown, however, that this is not always the case. Some PMOs are simply not staffed to provide that type of support.

Paid Mentoring/Coaching

If you don't have anyone to turn to for help, guidance, and support, an alternative is to pay someone to help you.

Finding the right mentor or coach, I think, is the challenge. There are lots of business coaches as well as consulting firms, but I'm not so sure about project management mentors/coaches. A quick search on Google will give you the answer.

All right, I'll put in a plug here: I offer one-on-one project management mentoring/coaching. You get dedicated time to assist you with defining and planning your projects as well as reviewing your progress and answering questions—for a fee, of course.

Once you get through one or two projects, you can fly on your own and maybe you can even pass on your knowledge to someone else.

Tips

Make sure you identify someone who can help you *before* you need the help.

Just Do It!

Knowing is not enough; we must apply. Willing is not enough; we must do.

—Johann von Goethe

Are you ready to bite the bullet?

Now that you have a pretty good idea of how to do this stuff, are you ready to apply what you have learned?

It's easier than you think

Remember that the process is simple:

1. Define what you're trying to do.

2. Come up with a plan to do it.

3. Get everyone focused.

4. Make sure the work gets done.

5. Handle the problems.

6. Deal with any changes.

7. Manage the team.

8. Keep everyone informed.

9. Wrap it up.

10. Celebrate.

Learn the process

It bears repeating; take a class or workshop to help you learn the process. The advantage of taking a class is that you can ask questions and get immediate answers and guidance as you work through the class.

Leverage templates and tools to make project management easier and faster

Use the worksheets that have been provided throughout the book or find other useful ones on the Internet.

Go to the "Resource" section of this book for the URL to the templates in this book.

As for tools, to start, use the ones you already have. Why waste time learning a new tool in addition to learning a new process?

Get support

If you're new at this, it does help to find someone who can answer your questions and listen to your ideas. Getting support will save you lots of frustration.

Now go forth!

So, just get started! You'll do fine. And if you get stuck or need help, you know where to find me.

And here's to your success!

About the Author

Juana Clark Craig is the Principal of Practical Guidance LLC. She is that rare individual who possesses warmth, humor, and openness and who is genuinely interested in helping others succeed.

She is a project management professional (PMP) with over twenty-five years of project management and project management office experience working for *Fortune* 500 companies.

Juana has personally managed projects ranging from tens of thousands of dollars to millions of dollars. She has extensive experience in helping organizations dramatically increase their project success rate through training, mentoring, and coaching new and experienced project managers.

Juana is passionate about project management and passionate about helping others achieve the results she knows that can be gained by using it.

She is a techno-geek at heart, an avid reader, and a researcher. She's a very practical person who likes things to be simple, straightforward, and to the point. Her philosophy and writing reflect her style.

Juana is happily married and has three children. She lives in Columbia, Maryland.

Resources

To access all the worksheets and templates presented in this book, please visit www.project-management-lite.com

Click "Resources" from the navigation menu.

Glossary of Terms

actuals - how much time or money was actually spent

assumption - something that you take for granted is true

budget - the total amount of money available for the project

change - something different from what it was before

constraint - a limitation

customer - an end consumer who will be using whatever it is you're delivering

deliverable - something you produce or perform

invoice - a bill from a vendor

issue - a concern or a problem that should be addressed

labor - people: staff, contractors, consultants, etc.

milestone - a significant event at a point in time

non-labor - non-people stuff like equipment and supplies

risk - a chance that something bad or good might happen in the future

sponsor - the person who's paying for/wants the project. You may have a project sponsor and an executive sponsor:

- The Project Sponsor is there (I hope) to help you navigate the political waters and make decisions about project direction and to help you resolve issues that you can't resolve yourself.

- The Executive Sponsor is the big cheese who wants the project. You want to keep him or her happy. The Executive Sponsor usually talks to the Project Sponsor to find out how things are going, but it would be a good idea for you to make contact.

stakeholder - a person who may be impacted by the project either positively or negatively. Knowing who's who would be a good idea. If you don't manage stakeholder expectations, these people can derail your efforts.

subject matter experts (SMEs) - the people who have in-depth knowledge about whatever the project is about (at least what's currently going on)

task - a piece of work that has to be done

team - the brain trust and worker bees who will be helping you to get the project done; take good care of the team

variance - the difference between values such as costs and dates

vendors - the people who sell you stuff such as products and services. Take whatever vendors say about pricing and schedules with a grain of salt. Read EVERYTHING. You've been warned!

Made in the USA
San Bernardino, CA
22 September 2016